FLOW
COMMOTION

By Tyler G. Freitas

Of Mere Being

The palm at the end of the mind,
Beyond the last thought, rises
In the bronze decor,

A gold-feathered bird
Sings in the palm, without human meaning,
Without human feeling, a foreign song.

You know then that it is not the reason
That makes us happy or unhappy.
The bird sings. Its feathers shine.

The palm stands on the edge of space.
The wind moves slowly in the branches.
The bird's fire-fangled feathers dangle down.

—Wallace Stevens

Contents

Acknowledgements

This collection has been substantially improved by the feedback and support from my dear friends, Patrick Lahey and P. Brady; my mentor, Mark Cotta Vaz; and my wife, Ariel. I feel indebted to my fellow Bay Area residents, for providing me with material and an alternative perspective on what it means to be a citizen who is dependent upon BART and our local transportation infrastructure. Thank you all for accompanying me on this journey.

Safe travels,

Tyler G. Freitas
November 2023

Part 1:

Heading to the station

Me Gusta Musica

Crypto

        is

           crash

              -ing

Yet, there's Mexican music and dancing
Family connection   everyone moves away
Nobody can afford to pay $10 a gallon

We

           lost

   immediacy
   attentiveness

For likes, facts, and quick laughs

A dopamine hit to the dome

It feels a bit like Rome—
right before collapse.

Portland

Poor souls living in tents
Scat-tered   about
Tattoos, piercings, neon hair

Willamette River slicing the city in two

No sales tax, clear skies, and tasty food

Crowds gather about, in protest
of the death of Roe vs. Wade

30 Years

We all knew
           the day would come
When we would
           lose our youth
No longer naive,
           but still very ignorant
Of a world's machinations
           domestic and foreign
Biopharma, MedTech . . . Tech-Tech

Greed, envy, consume, consume, consume
MUNCH MUNCH MUNCH MUNCH

Can't fill the void –
           won't pray til doom

Where did laughter and humility go?

Out the window, as we sit and stare at screens
Gripping our spleens, tainted by lab-made foods
Population growth—societal collapse
Waiting for the moment to lapse
Breath deep into the bottom of the lungs
The Game of Life has just begun.

Grand Prize

Can't
>   fall
without taking a step

Can't
>   fail
without trying

Can't breathe
>   in a vacuum

Can't see
until light hits the eye

We will die—
few will live

Give and get more
Cry tears of joy
Lay prostrate in unbelief
Release grief to relieve
Forgive first, then analyze
Love always, sidestep shadows,
presence is the prize.

Special Day

Flowers

        familiar faces

                Beautiful Bride

The culmination of love exploration

Tears of joy and boisterous laughs

Who knew a day could pass so fast

Sunsets never last.

One decision

        knocks

           the domino:

Catalyzing a relational experiment

Forming an unbreakable bond

Crossing the threshold—

Honey Doom

Lots of quaint shops in downtown Carmel
Casanova serves expensive, delicious food
It takes a few drinks to get into the mood:
Breaking through the shell's surface

Dreams of children—suffused by light
Masterful music by Freitas fills the night
Rich chocolate cake melts to the touch
Flocks of birds fly below and above

Take a trip down 17 Mile Road
People crowd the sites and expose

Tourists – why the fuck do you care?
Take a picture – hollow-eyed stares

Cruise to a desolate monarch grove
Gone til November – surely they'll return
Head to Monterey – poverty gathers about
Sitting atop
      the Ocean
        watching pale kayakers bob in the sea.

Off Course

An inept leader

           destroys faith

                among followers

Eventually, no compensation or incentive will
suffice
False niceties

           rotten rose petals

                        s c a t t

ered
Drunken pirates divulge dirty secrets
Plunder the company for resources and talent
Then set up shop across the street
Pray for a storm to sink your enemy's ship
Compassion is out of fashion – tongues lashing
Waves crashing against the hull – wind thrashing
Shifting from side-to-side

                will it hold?

Someone killed the Captain
Quick – write a caption.

Time Passes—Seasons Change

Suavesito Souldies
Downtown Oakland
Beers, beers, and cocktails
Familiar music for the first time
Sounds from my parents' generation
When the Nation was still proud
And enemies were easily seen

Skewed

Media

Reminds me that freedom has a cost
Most of us never see what's lost
Postmen and women are invisible—
Yet I still recall the face of my
childhood UPS driver

Now, I wonder what people think
Perverse motivations—hard to sleep

Weep!
    For those who stay pure,
    then lose it all, for days on end—
    we know kindness is a cure
    so children can play with friends—
    while adult relationships disintegrate.

Bored Deity

Let it be said

        when lies fill heads

Wrongs are forgotten

        is this true? Guess not.

Birds scream

        lakes dry

           people still love

Family and friends

persevere, pushed and shoved

From above

      is someone

        judging us?

An idle existence

        for God

           to pass eternity

Like watching ants . . .

        while paint dries.

A Seed of Truth

A seed was planted beneath the loam
Waiting in anticipation – all alone
In a brook, beside daffodils in bloom
Under the pale blue light of the moon

Yet, not a drop of water reached the ground
Dry and dying like Prometheus bound
Children laughed and played without sound
Season changed – the Earth spins round

Morning dew glistens, but won't suffice
Winter comes—turns lakes to ice
Drum taps quicken as ants prepare to fight
Enola Gay ascends with an island in sight

Break

       these

              infernal rhythms –

sanctimonious schisms

Let the Devil's minions scour the world
Proud angels descend, pinions unfurled
The battle rages eternally . . .
Beyond the narrow gaze of the faithless

Why did the first explorers perish?
Planks of wood floating like dead fish
A fevered Poet burns their papers
Truth never stood a chance – all was vapor.

Dilapidated

Who thought it was a good idea to let
a confused child
sit atop a trash pile,
soiling our green planet?

Religion looks inviting
when friends are fighting
and loved ones whisper secrets

Anxious about the future
obscuring our features
crawling with creatures—
listen to the preacher

A bitter fruit can be healing,
but the paint keeps peeling.

The Doubt Before Discovery

A little, brown dog is running along the road
I slow the car and search for an owner.
No one is nearby
should I call the pound?
Attempt to save the pup from passing cars—
or let it be, to chase tail, or flee:
from a neglectful home—welcome the scars
life spent locked away, starving and depraved
might be worse than an early grave.
Striding and striving for personal pursuits
      and the fruit of expended energy
nature grows toward the light
          bright, floral displays
spinning like a salsa dancer's dress
who am i to say
        whether a life is lost, or saved?

Beatnik Burial Ground

San Francisco is a ghost city
sewage steams up from the sidewalk
tech has fled to remote locations
dirty men limp by with hollow eyes
                where's the prize?
No pot of gold at the end of the road
lie down on the cold cement, as time flies
cells yearn for life, but the mind begs to die.
The Beats are gone, but City Lights stands—
a relic from a time when people still tried:
injustices attacked with retributive language
drink and drugs destroyed social programming
able hands grasped for more than TV remotes.
             Now, KTVU 2 spreads lies.

Part 2:

On BART/Commuting

In Transit

Teeth chattering on the Castro Valley BART
platform
Runny nose flows – waiting for the SF-bound
train.
It arrives
>   but the doors do not open
>   so, I hurry to a different car
all of the seats are taken
>   a large puddle covers the floor
>   it's not raining
passengers read, or stare at their phones—
>   avoiding eye contact of every passing
person
>   wishing for an earthquake to end the
rhythm
>   or a thief to steal my work equipment
anything to slow the pessimistic train of thought.
>   Today could be the day!
>   I arrive at my stop.

Late Night Ride

I walk into 19th Street station a little before 8 PM
      Nine people in the car:

      A black security guard
      A tattooed hipster couple
      A white guy with a mask at the back—
          scanning the surroundings,
          slipping his arm into his backpack

Doors close

      You know then that it is not the commute
      That makes us happy, or unhappy.
      The train moves. Its facade fades.

Rolling into Bay Fair without a care
      black guy with glasses and gray beanie
stares
      at the white and yellow passing lights.

Transfer trains.

Sleeping with the Sheep

A dirty man, sitting across the aisle, keeps
nodding off
      and dropping his phone
      he picks it up—
      two minutes later,
he drops it again—
the screen is severely cracked
every edge is splintered.
It has been a cold Winter
Apprehensive parents try to keep their kids
occupied

Don't stare at the dirty man!

We're all on a trip without a plan
      sit or stand – make demands
Blank faces drown the noise with headphones.
      The dirty man is all alone
      eyes close, then falls the phone
      he could put it in his pocket,
      but he needs to see the screen to sleep—
      hands are shaking, his high is fading.

19th Street Station

at 9PM on a Thursday night in January.
The loudspeaker is screeching—loudly
A person with a lot of denim,
        a black beard,
        pink hair,
and a bike with the Pride flag on the back
is sitting on the bench beside me.
      We tipsily talk about how strange it is
        to have so much money floating
around
      and yet our infrastructure is shrieking at
us;
      louder than the flatlining of a close loved
one—
A decrepit shamble of a City that was once proud
      before tech and biotech
      abused our senses,
      poisoning body and mind
some days I wish I were blind—
until I step on human shit on the sidewalk.

Artificial Flavoring

A black woman with a black jacket
and three small, silver ball lip piercings
walks passed me
  yelling, "Shut the fuck up."
   "Shut the fuck up!"
  "Come over here and sit down!"
Her daughter sits next to her in the corner.
Her son sits next to me.
The boy pulls out a basketball-themed snack
container
unzips it, and removes a blue-wrapped bar
he tears the wrapper with his teeth:
  releasing an artificial blueberry scent.
I feel like I'm supposed to help these kids,
  but then I arrive at my stop.

Part 3:

Arrival/Vacation

Equifinality

There's a thirty-year-old black man, starving,
because he spent all of his money feeding his dogs
so they can grow strong, and multiply,
so a child can have a puppy for Christmas.

There's a forty-year-old white man on the street
because he lost his job to a robot.
He fought hard, but now he smokes pot—
a discarded burrito is a tasty treat.

There's a fifty-year-old tenured college professor
sitting in an ivory tower with a tweed suit,
who has infrequent sex with his spouse,
only missionary style – empty rooms in the house.

There's a sixty-year-old government employee
who dreams of traveling to beautiful, exotic lands
but the monotony buries her head in the sand
and painful joints force her to waddle slowly.

There's a seventy-year-old retiree
who is beginning to lose their memory
so the family puts them in a lonely home
strangers sit in the room on their phones.

Run to Big Brother

Lay people, make way for the all-powerful
ChatGPT.
Close your word processors
        your savior has arrived.
Switch off your brain and stuff food in your
mouth
slovenly lie around and play video games on the
couch.
        Big brother will provide
        what AI deprived
Bureaucrats run and hide –
hold on for dear life,
til the pensions run dry.
Who wouldn't want to die after losing their
purpose?
Why crawl back to the spouse and hungry kids'
mouths?
Time to pack a small bag and head down South:
sit under a palm tree with a bird overhead
sucking on a mai thai the brain cells are dead.

Historical Forecast

The future is uncertain, the past is hazy—
the old are dying, youth want to be lazy.
Look strangers in the eyes, but not too long
head filled with lies, the Dark Side is strong—

Go, walk toward the waning light
slow and steady through the night
fight demons with all your might—
honest words while angered starts fights.

When money is abundant, and work is easy
life is a beach, and worries are fleeting.
Trapped in a castle, pitying the weak
The mob is restless, they take to the street.

Hope for the best, prepare for the worst
antiques appreciate, and new stuff breaks
rain is restorative, until the dam bursts
run through a red light, ready the hearse.

Taking Root

You came from far lands
      and landed amidst paradise,
but the strife of daily life is casting shade,
      depriving you of much needed vitamin D.
So, you'll have to settle for the moon
and hope that a monsoon doesn't wash you away,
out into the sea, suffocating, instead of setting
roots.
When the curtains close, we see the Truth:
actors get undressed backstage
            removing makeup
            switching masks
no one knows how long the interlude will last.
The last act has long passed –
      several seasons of leaves falling
fast.
Eventually, our species will be extinguished—
but for now, we're spreading seeds
fighting and toiling to make ends meet
helping friends steady their feet
when the next wind blows,
let go, fly free.

Skimming the Fat

After graduating from high school
A teenage girl went off to college
Honing her mind, avoiding the fools
A fox loaned her money for knowledge

Then she graduated with an Art degree
And got a job, because living isn't free:
Food, rent, and utilities—working like a bee
Then a fox came to collect the fee

Now she's married to a work horse named Fred
He builds hospitals for the living & morgues for
the dead
They decided to buy a house with a fence and a
gate
A fox from the department dropped when it got
late

A year later, their first kid ran about
And while working from home—she would shout
To quiet the kid, so she could sit in a meeting
A fox from the department was quietly eating

Eventually, the woman asked the fox,
"What is it that you do, exactly?"

"Well, we take your money to build roads and
schools."
"Then why are the roads crumbling, and the
children so dumb?"

The fox smirked and buttoned his expensive suit,
"I can't guarantee the efficiency of our system;
Not to mention the monkeys who need their
fruit."
The woman swiped at the fox, but sadly, she
missed him.

Black Friday Bargains

If I could turn water into wine
would I worry about quotidian tasks?
Make sure family and friends are fine—
gather the kids and stand in line.

Recession is in the air,
      but the deals make the herd stare:
shopping carts loaded to spread cheer
bloated bellies are bursting with beer
If I could walk on water
      would I be able to step below?
      would the water even touch my toe?
      no one knows.
Yet, we cling to favorite stories and allegories,
because it makes the days pass for a purpose.
One day, deeds will be weighed—
      who wants to be found wanting?

A Trip to Fresno

Leaving the East Bay,

                      heading toward Fresno

After 30 minutes of driving East

the surroundings flatten

                  flat_

Punctured by orchards

                  flat_

                  orchard^^^

Pass by several "Pray for Rain" signs

Spirituality and religion are great

for the rich and ignorant, respectively.

The parched yellow soil gasps for a drop

It rained yesterday for a moment , , ,

Now, the light blue sky is filled with

                  white popcorn clouds.

All of the cities along the way look the same

Giant gas station signs reach from behind trees

Two- and three-lane highways all the way

Nearly smashed against a cement partition

                  by several semi trucks

Stop at Valero to relieve myself

                  and put $20 in the tank

Grab lunch in downtown Fresno

              and park in the nearly empty lot.

Only a few people are on the street
Grimacing faces and boarded buildings
I walk to a bar . . . three patrons inside
The bartender tells me that he just
kicked out a big black woman who
was smoking crack in the men's restroom.

I ask him, "Is there anything to do or see?"

"No, but there's plenty to drink."

Imminent

I

Hurry now, child,
                 be free
live each day in ecstasy.

Take a trip to Mexico
                 move slow
watch the blades of grass grow.

Sail South to Panama
                 cross the canal
buy a bundle of bananas.

Run amongst the palm trees
                 feel the breeze—
the ship rocks rhythmically.

Dark clouds form in the north
                 steel thyself
crumbs fall from empty shelves.

Rest your head in the shade
                 tides change
war is here, nowhere to run.

II

The sky is filled with smoke
        the ranks have broke
bullets fly, bodies lie, eyes are closed.

Vultures circle in anticipation
        land in the sand,
curved beaks make lacerations.

Bombs explode throughout the night
        try to sleep—
pierced and painted by morning light.

Stiff limbed, with broken bones
        soldiers stagger home
the land has changed, trees have grown.

The child stares, but doesn't recognize
        changed by sins
heavy burdens cause caving in.

Buried beneath a pile of memories
        no air to breathe
clawing the earth til fingers bleed.

III

The war is over, finished, done
               and although we won
we lost a lot of daughters and sons.

Stars explode lightyears away
               nuns gather to pray
time gives way to brighter days.

Brittle joints crack and creak
               wrinkly feet
grandchildren laugh in the hall.

Don't fall now, the trials have passed
               work is done
savor each drop until the last.

Retire and recline amongst the palms
               gold bird on the frond
the wind blows away all qualms.

Prepare the ground, loosen the dirt
               it won't hurt
go to sleep in your favorite shirt.

Paradise Village

Obese Midwesterners and Canadians
                    stare past
the obsequious Mexican service staff.

Cold beer and sugary cocktails
            dribble down their mouths
plates of nachos and tacos pile high.

The activity crew get people moving
                    but not too much
no one wants a cardiac event.

Don't bother speaking Spanish
                this is vacation—
not the time for foreign relations.

I believe these people are good
                cultured? No.
This isn't where the celebrities go.

I learned how to swim in these pools
                happy memories
buried in the sand for eternity.

Bingo by the Pool

Two alligators are staring at me
    with open mouths.
Laura is organizing bingo
fifteen people float in the water
1,300 pesos for the winner
     "G 39"
     "O 65"
a fat woman in a turquoise one-piece
    eases into the hot tub
a volleyball flies through the air
    waves break along the rocks
     "BINGO!"
a child slides out of the alligator's mouth.

Outer Bodies

Flying north in economy class
　　　　toward the cold Bay.
Home, after a week away,
　　　　to a boring job and mob.
Drug-filled City streets weep
too much trash for weekly sweeps
intelligent people glare at screens
time passes in pointless meetings . . .
lose sleep to deadlines,
　　　　and loved ones to disease
relationships aren't able to bloom
snack wrappers cover the room
bellies extend, hairs gray, kids play . . .
　　　　　　on phones and pads
mom and dad stare at each other
　　　　hollow-eyed – love extinguished
blackened rose petals break off
　　　　in this painful, dark dream.

Avaricious Avians

An unattended salad on a lounge chair,
             beside a beach palapa,
attracts pencil-beaked, black birds.

Four or five of them peck about
             devastating the caesar,
then they stop to scan for the falconer.

Of Mere Extinguishing

You struck a spark in my heart
      illuminating dreams obscured in the dark.
And as time slipped by
            like a parade procession
The formerly towering economy runs toward
recession—
Feelings swell, then the tides begin their
regression:
Trivialities and pains that went unsaid
           screamed from steaming
heads
And the initials carved in the tree trunk
           are covered by
bark.
Subtle idiosyncrasies stab the senses
         sewing a tapestry of
discontent.
In the end, after it bursts into flames
      the fire-fangled phoenix will not rise
again.

Filling

Two grandparents passed away before I was born
Then two surrogate grandparents in middle
school
So much potential love stripped away at an early
age

        parts of my identity remained a mystery
what wisdom would they have shared with me?
Opaque recollections obscure like a dense fog
              they would watch me play
and grow
so many things to say and show
I know there will be a time
to meet in astral space
swirling stardust
reversing the years of rust
filling the loss with love.

Dipsea Trail

Standing atop the mountain, with the Pacific to
the west
       and the sun shining to the east
          bathing the valley with
orange-yellow light.
My friends says, "Look at that!"
I stare in the same direction
       at the sea of redwoods above and below
          and nod in affirmation.
The friend comments, "The air is so refreshing."
I take a deep breath in solidarity.
Gorgeous homes perched on the mountainside
       with tall rooms and floor-to-ceiling
windows
and occupants who have lost interest in the
scenery.
The Bay and spanning bridges carrying cars across
       away from the monotony and doldrums of
daily life.
My wife was barely visible when I awoke at 5:30,
but her beauty and fragrance were boundless.

"I think that his function is to make his imagination theirs and that he fulfills himself only as he sees his imagination become the light in the mind of others. His role, in short, is to help people to live their lives."
—Wallace Stevens, "The Noble Rider and the Sound of Words"

Unnatured

Oh, noble poet, can you still see the light?
Do not let the world's worries weigh you down—
observe, embrace your innate empathic tendency
  allow space for vulnerability and
connection
avoid judging those who wander by
  lie on the grass and let the mind fly.
Nature's hum reminds us of life's rhythms
  dense minerals bind to form prisms:
fractals and geometry defined from the beginning
  shapes and size confined by their limits
exquisite chemicals dance on our tongues
  sweet scented flowers bathe under the sun
this land used to be fruitful and filled with
game—
  today, the streets are paved, and homes are
plain.

Where the Wild Things Died

I finished *The Ohlone Way* today
       It's a cloudy day in the Bay.
I wonder, what was it like in the Spanish
Missions?
       Baptized by an old, robed Franciscan
monk
Subjected to Latin lessons and rigorous prayer
rituals
A single God—as opposed to numerous animal
deities.
The unmarried women were locked away
While Western diseases spread in the windowless
room
If you could escape, they'd send troops
Tearing children from parents like plants from
roots.
Trained to make clothes that are climatically
ineffectual
Laborious agricultural practices in a land of
abundance
Whips crack on the backs of dissidents
Father Serra self-flagellates for his failures.
"Why won't these beastly beings run toward
reason?

Embrace our ways—forget about the acorn
season."
Then, in 1834, after the Mexicans closed the
Missions,
		the Anglos arrived, and slaughtered them
Courts wouldn't listen—aliens on their own land
Peace and kindness were never part of the plan.

Franklin

My dog has few possessions:
a tennis ball, a cylindrical red squeaker,
an orange frisbee, soccer ball, and two blankets.
       If you pick one up, he will come up to you
And if you don't throw it—he'll jump and whine.
Toss it, he might bring it back; until he gets bored.
Cats, chickens, squirrels – chase them away!
The territorial boundaries are demarcated
When foreigners come near, queue the barking
And if there's nothing to do, he'll sleep all day
Then, when someone moves, he'll open an eye,
            but continue to snore.
I think he thinks that sleeping causes others to
move:
       The world is waiting for him to start
dreaming—
Preparing the stage and putting the actors in place
       And when the curtain rises, he's ready to
play.

Operating Procedures

Lie about your qualifications.
Kiss your manager's ass.
      Don't work too hard.
The company is the enemy;
a piggy bank to bust open
and plunder for the bi-weekly
      ration of bacon.
Complain about every task.
Gossip about colleagues.
Always act busy –
      move your mouse.
Don't act too complacent.
Leave work incomplete for review;
make your bosses feel valued.
Curse the competition every day.
Criticize disagreeable customers.
YOU are always right, but be quiet.
Brag about your accomplishments.
Celebrate mundane achievements.
Push deficiencies into the corner
      of the storage closet.
The CEO is here to speak,
On your feet!
      Straighten your tie!
Nod . . . smile, lie.

Book Crooks

I used to sell my worn paperbacks to the used
book store;
the same store that I bought them at a few months
before.

> *Catch-22, The Plague, Tortilla Flat*
> $2.99 each

And when I took them home

    I would unfold the dog-eared pages

    and erase remarks written in pencil,

    accumulating roughly ten titles before

journeying back:
standing in line for my turn to speak to the sickly
clerk.
And when I go to collect my pittance,
the salesperson informs me that several books are
worthless.

Ruined

Vituperative insult spit from abusive lips
        strikes the core:
        reddening cheeks
            unable to speak
the door to thought slams shut.
Honor stained like blood on a surgeon's smock.
        Women gawk.
        Children stare.
            Blake's Vision is clear:
loathsome deeds that ears cannot unhear.
The rain and wind lash the home
eroding the stepping stones
unsettling the foundation
war breaks out
sacrifice life to save face, and nation.

Adonde Deus

Every time I go to downtown Oakland
and San Francisco
I search for God: High
        and low.
There are fingerprints on the buildings
     bodies laying about
     and shit on the sidewalk—
     all smeared and smudged.
The deities have abandoned the cities
and they took the good souls, too.
Young, beautiful tech professionals gossip
       outside Salesforce's tower.
When I ask the local inhabitants,
     "Where did Deus go?"
     They don't know.
I try to paint a picture:
     a beautiful, renaissance piece—
     but they just fart and shrug,
"There's no bearded man above
nor a red, horned beast below,
     and Buddha is a big, bald braggart!"
I sigh –
stare through the charcoal concrete jungle,
and ask, "What did the City do to you?"

Extremes

So much hate and rage
      drugs
            deaths
                  disasters
Kids don't go out any more,
      because it isn't safe,
            depravity lurks in every corner—
The news tells us to be afraid
      locked away:
Staring at cell phone screens, and screaming TVs
      censoring and silencing dissidents
          exploiting privacy
          anything to preserve our not so
united states.
Of course the kids would rather play video games
      and watch porn – lots of it.

But in quiet places, people venture out:
              rebuilding
        rebirthing
    resting
So much love and peace.
Kids dance, laugh, and play
      generations gather
          happiness grows every day.
It's okay to look the other way

set yourself free:

    spend time in serenity.

Day by Day

A girl is born in the mountains to two
          capable and intelligent parents
surrounded by books and trees
          she's strong and resilient.
Another girl is born in the suburbs
        to a surprised man and a ditsy woman
surrounded by booze and weed
        she's squirming like a caterpillar.
Who can say definitively which child will thrive
          and live a life worthy of envy?
Fame and misfortune are dealt without
discernment,
        inflated egos rise and burst in the sun
        a speeding car will sunder anyone.

Linguiça

It looks like a large, long red hot dog
        but it is much spicier
        and the yellow-orange fat seeping out
           burns like hell.

Put it in a bun, add a little mustard
        and you're good to go.

Be careful, though
        your burps will burn
        your stomach might turn
run to the bathroom
        you're ready to blow.

Data Limitations

Try to copy me

        ChatGPT,

       any AI.

There's no reason to my rhymes.

Life is sublime.

Life evolves.

Times change,

        things move,

                start anew.

Whatever I've written is done

        (sparsely revised)

Go ahead and

        imitate –

              I've already

moved on.

Pay Attention

Spring has arrived
       birds are chirping
              bunnies are hopping
                     the sun is shining.
Children are laughing and playing—
       go outside on such an idyllic day.
No inane email chains,
       from scammers and solicitors.
Some people work 15 hour days
       the pay is okay, but time tics on—
We can never replace grains atop the hour glass—
       how long does a child's cry, or laugh, last?
Or were you,
like me,
scared of the traffic;
       the stressed parents & dark-eyed
adolescence?
School ended ten years ago, but I'm still in session:
       teachers are talking, but I don't listen to
the lessons.

The Colonizer

Your body is the property of the State:
>Hair, eyes, teeth, toes, and skin.
We will burn most of it, and stretch
>the latter across the continent
>to remind the remaining Natives:
Your land is the property of the State:
>Mountains, plains, forests, and rivers.
We will exploit the ground and toss your viscera
>into the streams for the fish to feast upon,
>and force your children to watch—
so they never dream of roaming free.

Written in response to *This Wound is a World* by Billy-Ray Belcourt (2017).

Part 4:

Returning

Deliverance

The old BART trains screech and shake
　　　rusty, worn wheels grind against the rails
faded plastic seats are indented and wrinkled
　　　paint is scratched off the walls
　　　windows are covered with a film of dirt
people cover their face with masks—
　　　for Covid, or to avoid the stench of
occupants?
I couldn't say.
I pray to a God that I don't believe in, to forestall .
. .
　　　seismic activity:
　　　liquefying cement pillars
　　　suspended in the air
　　　　　swaying like a palm in a storm
　　　careening, screaming,
falling.

Stationary

Wendy's

   Chevron

      San Leandro Station

Emergency Evacuation | Safety Information

streetlights – headlights

     poorly lit buildings

        red stop lights

semi truck

tail lights

right blinker

ARCO

    Ross

        Bayfair Mall

Bayfair Station

    "10 car train for San Francisco"

bicycle leaned against the back seat

    asian man playing a phone game

indian man searching Google

      Three Crosses.

A Thursday in March

A middle-aged woman speaking Spanish on the
phone departs.
The woman who was sitting next to her returns to
her seat
and puts her huge, white bag of plastic bottles
next to her.
Two masked Asian men speak quietly . . .
       the sole of a black, red, and white Nike is
staring at me.
Woke people expend time and money to shop
ethically—
       to spare disadvantaged people from cruel
labor—
       stripping away their opportunity for
social mobility.
Children mine cobalt in the Congo
       so stupid people can stare vacantly at their
smart phones.
An Indian woman boards, sits down,
       and scans about suspiciously.

Relax

They say, "Relax, it will be okay."
Brazil, Russia, India, China, and South Africa
                                 join forces.
ChatGPT is improving every day
          wiping out white collar workers.
Automate, automate, automate.
No need for lazy employees.
3D print micro apartments, then lock the doors
self-driving cars will deliver goods from stores.
Send the billionaires to the space station,
                       and Musk to Mars.
Psychological scars are visible in every BART car—
baggy clothes and burnt blunts—we're in the Bay.
Language changes, cities too, interest rises, what
to do?
Don't pity the person sleeping on the manhole
cover—
                   soon, it could be you.

Corrupção

Walking around San Francisco on 4/20
      weed wafting through the air.
Working and talking at company parties
      lots of smiles, but nobody cares.
Bartenders pour strong drinks
      the City stinks.
Vacant offices stare down at the people
      huddled masses are unconscious,
        tucked into corners.
Go to BART before eleven
      a white woman in black and white joggers
      scans the platform – head shifting
side-to-side
we board the train, she sits behind.
It seems that she has made a friend;
      they talk about fentanyl and prescription
schemes.
The friend brags about the boxes of clothes,
      bras, and undergarments that she stole
from Ross.
My buddy works at Ross.
To steal and deal drugs is one thing
      but to brag,
while people lose their jobs,
      is sickening.

White Fright

The 7:12AM train arrives at CV.

> A short, white man runs out, to the car
behind.
I step into the cabin –

> there's a wheelchair filled with
blankets,

> and a sticker on the side that says,
> Legalize LSD.

There's no owner in sight –

> then a black man with dreads and Ninja
Turtle socks

> enters the cabin from the car in front.

He's pacing about,
while continuously delivering a soliloquy.
I have earbuds in,

> so I only see his lips moving, and his
raving eyes

> there's a palpable tension on the train:

why the fuck is this guy going so hard before 8AM?

> is what everyone is thinking, but no one
will say.
Eventually, three policemen board our car,

> the *offender* peacefully gathers his
belongings,
and I'm sad, because he made so much open space.

Gatekeeper

The BART car's doors aren't closing
        someone is standing in the way
                holding the door for late friends
                        who probably wouldn't
return the favor.
It's after 5PM
        all of the passengers are restless
                a few begin to shout,
                        "Get out of the way!"
After three failed closing attempts,
        the friends finally arrive—
                the perpetrator confronts an
angry asian woman
                        arguing,
insulting—everyone stares silently.
Nobody wants to deal with the aftermath
        the potential hair pulling, slapping, and
wrestling
                the train is stuffy, and we're
exhausted
                        San Francisco sucked the
life from our souls.
Now, Oakland is stomping us into the ground
        the A's are moving away—I'm dismayed
                at a loss for what to say . . .

Parental Indifference

The kids are mentally sick,
  addicted to the chronic—
    instead of hooked on phonics.
Scrolling through smartphones
  watching hella pornos
    itching for that ringtone.
Parents grab the bottle
  and fly off the rails—
    they should've let go of the
throttle.
Better keep the kids inside
  let them stay high,
    then they'll fear the outside.
If we cannot trust each other
  and listen to learn—
    men will never be brothers.
People will hang dirty laundry
  for the whole world to see:
    the children are gone—where
could they be?

The Shitty

BART is canceling trains
　　　　SF is extending paid parking hours
　　　　　　　two more reasons to avoid the
Shitty.
People complain about the stench
　　　　of homeless people –
　　　　　　　forcing them into another car.
SF tried to legislate affordable housing—
　　　　projects do not pencil out
　　　　　　　white flight doesn't happen
overnight.
I can still recall idyllic days in the City:
　　　　driving down Lombard Street
　　　　　　　walking around Pier 39.
Skyscrapers shining, the future was bright—
then came the tech tax havens—
　　　　　　　now, techies flee from their leases.
Money moves to wherever it grows—
culture and creativity were killed years ago,
　　　　　　　desecrated by greed and poor
policies.